SCOTT FRANCIS

STUDY SKILLS FOR AMBITIOUS SENIOR STUDENTS

The High-Performance Advantage of the 8 Superhabits of Study

Copyright © Scott Francis 2023

All rights reserved. No part of this book may be reproduced or transmitted in any form or by any means, electronic or mechanical, including photocopying, recording or by any information storage and retrieval system, without prior permission in writing from the publisher.

Published in 2023

Published by Amba Press
Melbourne, Australia
www.ambapress.com.au

Cover designer – Tess McCabe
Editor – Beth Browne

ISBN: 9781922607584 (pbk)
ISBN: 9781922607591 (ebk)

A catalogue record for this book is available from the National Library of Australia.

Introduction

Introduction – Life Is Too Short for Bad Study	4
Superhabit 1 – The High-Performance Habit of an A+ Effort in Class	10
Superhabit 2 – The High-Performance Habit of Single-Tasking	18
Superhabit 3 – The High-Performance Habit of Setting Goals	24
Superhabit 4 – The High-Performance Habit of Using Practice Questions	32
Superhabit 5 – The High-Performance Habit of Sleep	40
Superhabit 6 – The High-Performance Habit of Spaced Practice	48
Superhabit 7 – The High-Performance Habit of Weekly Planning and To-Do Lists	56
Superhabit 8 – The High-Performance Habit of a Deliberate Mindset	64
Habits in Practice – A Deliberate Technique for Exams and Assignments	74
Habits in Practice – From the Pomodoro Technique to 'Flow'	84
Habits in Practice – Learning from Feedback	92
Habits in Practice – Mind Maps and Flashcards	98
Habits in Practice – Challenging Procrastination	106
References	114

Introduction
Life Is Too Good for Bad Study

"Life doesn't have to be perfect to be wonderful."
— Anette Funicello,
American actress and singer (1942–2013)

Introduction

If I could do one thing, it would be to encourage students to stop doing bad study. Bad study includes study that is distracted by social media, studying while extremely tired or studying while concentration is hard (perhaps after receiving some bad news).

Study under those conditions – distraction, fatigue or distress – is challenging and unlikely to lead to useful learning.

It would be much better to step away, do something else, have a nap, talk to someone, and come back later when the study conditions are better for learning.

There are two reasons that stepping away from bad study is worth thinking about:

1. You are not likely to be getting useful learning out of your study session.
2. The more time you spend doing ineffective study, the more you are going to dislike the process of study.

There are so many exciting things in the world that are not study, such as friendships, getting out in nature, hobbies, spending time with family, having a part-time job, playing sport and making music – the list goes on. If you are taking time away from these exciting elements of your life to study, my suggestion is that you should make sure that study is effective so it's a worthwhile use of your time.

Great study is a way to value your time.

As an academically ambitious student, this might be the first and most important mindset you adopt, that life is too good for bad study. Lean into this mindset and you might:

- challenge yourself to find study environments that are free of distractions
- challenge yourself to find effective times to study when you are not too tired or too busy
- challenge yourself to leave your mobile phone outside your study room, separate yourself from social media and close your email
- challenge yourself, on the days when study is difficult, to have a break, refocus, and get back to effective study.

After all, life is too good for bad study!

Introducing the 8 Superhabits of Study

A number of years ago I set myself a challenge – could I put the most important elements of study into a diagram that was simpler than the long presentations students often had to sit through about study skills.

The following diagram does that.

It has the 8 best habits I think a student who wants to be efficient with their time – and we all should want to be efficient with our time – should develop.

The diagram also tries to remind us of three other things:

1. A favourite saying of mine, that 'Life is too Good for Bad Study' – if you are making the commitment to study, do it well!
2. A reminder that study is not just about the time you put it, it is also about the effort you put into your study time. In fact, I think your study impact will be a mix of the time you put in, and the effort and focus while you work. I think of if as a maths formula: 'Study Impact = Intensity of Effort x Time'.
3. Study is about growing positive impact over time. I think of the analogy of a tree, that grows over time. Taking on a positive study habit will help water the 'tree' that represents growth as a learner.

We will learn more about the 8 habits, or superhabits as I call them, in this book. The diagram from the challenge I set myself to represent my most important ideas about study is opposite.

Superhabit 1
The High-Performance Habit of an A+ Effort in Class

"Everything we do is practice for something greater than where we currently are. Practice only makes for improvement."

— Les Brown,
American motivational speaker

The Basics

Part of me feels a touch fraudulent having the first chapter of a book that looks at the high-performance elements of study as one that encourages you to make the most of time in class (or lectures, tutorials or whatever formal classes you have for your learning). In a world of fascinating and sophisticated strands of research relating to learning, it seems to be an underwhelming place to start. However, it is important.

Time in class is spent in an environment with a unique mix of resources, including peers, a teacher, online resources and tangible resources like textbooks.

The best analogy for class time might be that it is the foundation of the other elements of learning, including study. The more you get out of your scheduled class time, the greater the insight you have into the topic you are learning by the time you come to start studying – a great advantage in the process of learning.

There are four high-performance questions you might want to use as a benchmark for considering how well you approach your time in class. To what extent are you:

- preparing before class?
- sitting with people who support your learning?
- practising active notetaking during class time?
- engaged in the class activities, including asking questions, giving answers and listening to other questions and answers?

Before moving on to the next section, let's consider notetaking as a specific learning skill that is worth being deliberate about. Notetaking seems to be an activity that increases in prevalence the further you move through your education, education, particularly in many senior high school classes and university lectures, where the focus can be on writing down notes. As such, building an effective strategy for taking notes can be an important part of getting the most out of class time.

Mueller and Oppenheimer (2014) consider that there might be two advantages from taking handwritten (rather than typed) notes. The first is that writing on a piece of paper creates fewer distractions – there are no incoming emails or alerts from social media. The second is that written notetaking might allow easier processing of information by underlining keywords or drawing a link between related concepts. Typed notes usually have more of the content written down and therefore tend toward the rewriting of content. It is worth being aware of this research, so that whether you are handwriting or typing notes you will be best served by doing it in an environment free of distractions and by highlighting, rewriting and finding and emphasising links in your notes wherever possible.

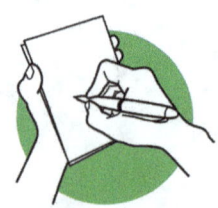

Beyond the Basics – Thinking High-Performance (with a Touch of Economic Theory)

To understand the opportunity of time spent in class, I want to introduce a sophisticated economic concept, that of opportunity cost.

Opportunity cost is what is given up to participate in an opportunity. It is an economic theory, so let's use an economic example to illustrate it.

Consider a retail business that has had a profitable year. They have a surplus of $10 million to invest in their business. The two options they are considering are opening another store or renovating their main store. They have only enough money to do one or the other. If they choose to renovate their main store, the opportunity cost (what they give up) is the opportunity to open a new store.

The idea of opportunity cost is relevant to your time in class in this way: generally there is not a lot that you have to give up to be in class. Your friends are also likely to be in class, and it is during the week, so there are not a lot of recreational activities on. There is not a lot to give up to be in class – or, to put it in economic terms, the opportunity cost of being in class is low.

Compare this with study on a weekend. Friends are out and about, the beach is packed, there are specials at the shop and chances to catch up with family – there are a whole lot of alternate activities that you could be involved with – or, to again use an economic term, the opportunity cost of study on the weekend is high.

Not only is the classroom (or lecture theatre or tutorial room) an environment rich with resources, it is also a relatively low opportunity cost environment.

Where Do We See this Habit in Other Environments?

If excellence is a habit (which it is), then students must consistently play in ways that are fundamentally excellent nearly all the time.

– Professor Robert A. Duke,
Head of Music and Human Learning, University of Texas

Gerald Klickstein (2009) wrote an article on the 7 habits of excellence for musicians. The last two habits caught my eye:

- focused attention – be alert in the practice room
- positive attitude – it takes time and diligence to acquire skills.

If we can bring focused attention and a positive attitude into the classroom, paralleling the habits of excellence of a musician, this will serve us well.

Any Boring Research to Support This?

Kassarnig, Bjerre-Nielsen, Mones, Lehmann and Lassen (2017) did an interesting study that tracked university students through their phones. They looked at more than 1000 students and came to two key conclusions:

1. Early and consistent class attendance strongly correlates with academic performance.
2. Attendance among social peers is substantially corelated with academic performance – if your friends show up, this helps encourage and improve your results.

These two findings are interesting to transfer to our discussion on getting the most out of class time. If showing up to university classes is such a positive for academic performance, then it makes sense that showing up to class with a determination to make the most out of class time will support effective learning. One of the factors we might be able to control in class is sitting with students who make us better as learners, and the results around peer influence suggest this is a factor worth being mindful of.

A Final Word

When it comes to being in class, you are there, the resources that you need are there and there are not many other opportunities demanding your attention. If you are motivated toward excellent learning outcomes, building a strong foundation in class will serve you well.

Superhabit 2
The High-Performance Habit of Single-Tasking

"By prevailing over all obstacles and distractions, one may unfailingly arrive at his chosen goal or destination."

– Christopher Columbus,
Italian explorer (1451–1506)

The Basics

Distractions are a modern enemy to effective work, including the work of study.

The prevalence of social media, mobile phones, email and other technology means that a level of intent is needed to find an environment where working without distraction is possible.

The simple reality is that multi-tasking, the opposite of single-tasking, reduces our capacity for learning.

In contrast, when we are single-tasking we give ourselves the best opportunity for learning.

Research suggests that single-tasking while we study allows us to recall information better, complete tasks more quickly and be more effective tackling complex tasks, all while experiencing less stress.

Beyond the Basics – Thinking Distractions and High Performance

I want to propose an activity for you to try – an activity that I have seen demonstrated a number of times.

To start with, time yourself doing the following task: spell the word 'multi-tasking' as quickly as you can and then count as quickly as you can from 1 to 12. Most people seem to take around 3 to 4 seconds to do this task.

Then do the same task again, but this time start with the first letter, then the first number, then the second letter, then the second number – so this time it is M 1 U 2 L 3 etc. Most people seem to take 12 seconds or more to do this.

Multi-tasking – in this case, switching between spelling and counting – seems to make the task take about three times as long.

In the book *Your High-Performance Guide to Study and Learning* (Francis and Nagel, 2020) Associate Professor Michael Nagel wrote that there is growing evidence that multi-tasking can lead to increased anxiety, negatively impact memory, inhibit creative thinking and lead to more mistakes – all of which are not great outcomes when you are studying.

Where Do We See this Habit in Other Environments?

Tania Miller is an orchestra conductor who wrote an article titled 'Harnessing Your Highest Potential in Performance'. It is an interesting insight into the world of high performance in the context of musical performance.

It goes without saying that distractions during rehearsals cannot be tolerated – there are no phones or social media during rehearsal time.

Miller goes further than this and makes the link between flow and distractions. Flow is a topic that is discussed later in this book. It refers to the times when performance – it might be athletic performance, creative performance or study performance – seems to come easily and with little conscious effort.

The following quote from Miller (2020) is well worth thinking about in the context of managing distraction as we sit down to study:

> *Everything is played in flow, there's no time to look back or think about anything other than the present moment …*
>
> *Performance in sport is similar … Those that can get into the mental zone of focus and confidence will have a greater chance of reaching their potential. Those that are distracted or worried don't have a chance.*

Any Boring Research to Support This?

There is an increasing body of research supporting the idea that multi-tasking reduces study effectiveness. Because phones are the gateway to social media, email and an inexhaustible supply of cat videos, they take pride of place as a key source of student distraction. I want to focus on research that highlights just how distracting phones can be.

Ward, Duke, Gneeze and Bos (2017) carried out a research project that demonstrates the value of managing distractions when you study. They focused on whether just the presence of a smartphone, with notifications turned off, reduced cognitive capacity. That is, they were interested in whether a phone with notifications turned off could negatively impact the mental processes that take place in the brain.

They asked the participants in their research study to place their phone either on the desk, in their laptop bag or in the next room.

The results? The further study participants were away from their phone – even with notifications turned off and not checking their phones at all – the better the participants performed on tests.

This suggests that not only do explicit distractions from phones, such as responding to a text message, pose a challenge while we study, but so do the distractions posed by just having a phone in the room with us.

A Final Word

These first two chapters have posed questions along the lines of: 'What is the price you are prepared to pay as a student?'.

In your quest for better learning, are you prepared to make an extra effort to get the most from class time?

In your quest for better learning, are you prepared to study in an environment without distractions (including from your phone and social media)?

Superhabit 3
The High-Performance Habit of Setting Goals

"Setting goals is the first step in turning the invisible into the visible."

– Tony Robbins,
motivational speaker and author

The Basics

Setting goals is a strategy that you might use to help focus your study efforts.

We tend to think of setting an academic goal as something we might do at the start of a semester. For example, we might set the goal of getting an A in maths.

A common goal-setting framework is to set a SMART goal. So the goal to get an A in maths might look like:

Specific:	Get an A in maths by the end of the semester.
Measurable:	Finish the semester with an A on my report card for maths.
Actions:	I will attend tutoring and spend an extra 30 minutes each weekend revising.
Realistic:	It requires improvement from a B to an A, so it seems realistic with extra work.
Timeframe:	The effort starts from week 1 and continues over the semester.

As we will see in the 'boring research' part of this chapter, setting goals is a habit associated with improved performance across a number of settings, including with study and learning.

Beyond the Basics – Thinking Goals and High-Performance

For some time I worked as a teacher at Bowen State High School in North Queensland. At the time, a mate of mine, Lyndon, was an assistant coach for the professional basketball team in Townsville, the Townsville Crocodiles. I was fortunate enough to be able to watch the team prepare for games, and I was interested in the way multiple goals were used to guide performance. The big players had goals around rebound counts, the guards around turnovers and the team around defensive efforts.

This leads to the first application of goals beyond setting a semester level goal. What if, for every study session you sat down to do, you had a clear goal or intent in mind? If goals help guide performance, why not jot down a clear intent every time you study? If nothing else, the feeling of satisfaction as you tick off that intent as complete will remind you of your progress. A goal you might have when sitting down to a study session could be to summarise several pages of a textbook, to find key references for an assignment or to write some practice questions for an upcoming exam.

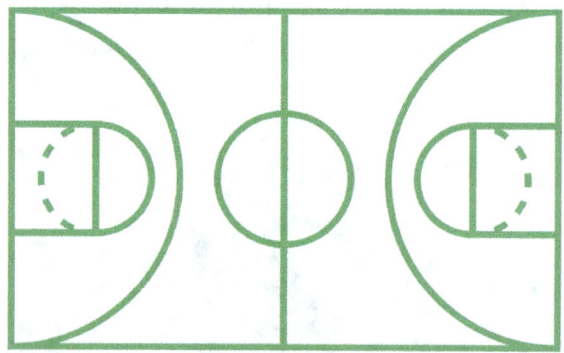

There is an interesting strand of research around the idea of open goals. This is a different goal-setting approach than a SMART goal, and my feeling is that it has value in an educational setting. In the pursuit of high-performance learning outcomes, it might be worth considering.

An open goal is one where the focus is on how well you can do. Rather than use a SMART goal for my maths to improve to an A, the focus would be to improve my maths result as much as I can over the semester. This addresses one of my key concerns with SMART goals: if you aim to improve from a B to an A but only get an A–, is that seen as a failure rather than a success? Research into open goals has also found that they are associated with more enjoyment, less stress and a greater sense of accomplishment. Next time you set a goal, consider using an open goal.

Where Do We See this Habit in Other Environments?

Francesca Egay (2022) wrote an article about two people whose goal was to write a book. Motivational speakers Jack Canfield and Mark Hansen decided in the 1980s that they wanted to write a book that was a collection of 101 inspirational stories. Their goal was concrete enough that they had a title for the book, *Chicken Soup for the Soul*, which was aimed at making readers feel comfortable.

Up until 1992 they had their book rejected 114 times. However, they persisted in working toward their goal and, that year, a small publisher took them on. Their idea was popular with readers, and there are now more than 250 titles in the series with over 500 million books sold worldwide – an extraordinary success.

A goal, persistence, and a remarkable success story.

Any Boring Research to Support This?

Edwin Locke is considered the pioneer in research around goal-setting theory. Over his career he found that the setting of challenging goals reliably led to improvements in performance. He summarised the evidence in a 2002 paper he wrote with Gary Latham:

> With goal-setting theory, specific difficult (challenging) goals have been shown to increase performance on well over 100 different tasks involving more than 40,000 participants in at least eight countries working in laboratory, simulation, and field settings.

Mark Murphy (2018) is a researcher who encourages us to consider writing down our goals, saying that the step of writing a goal increases the likelihood of it being achieved by 20% to 40%.

To summarise this research: setting a challenging goal, and writing it down, is an effective habit when looking to increase performance.

A Final Word

As a habit that guides improved performance, setting written goals for your work over a semester, as well as objectives when you sit down to study, are strategies that make sense.

Superhabit 4
The High-Performance Habit of Using Practice Questions

"Practice does not make perfect. Only perfect practice makes perfect."

– Vince Lombardi,
American football coach (1913–1970)

The Basics

One of the challenges for students understanding study skills is the use of (I think) unnecessarily complex language that researchers use around the topic. This chapter centres around one of those unnecessarily complex words: retrieval.

Retrieval, or retrieval practice, refers to finding information from your memory.

For example, if I ask you the following multi-choice question:

What is the lowest permanent court in the Queensland court hierarchy?

a. *Magistrates Court*
b. *District Court*
c. *Supreme Court*
d. *High Court*

You might recognise the answer as *(a) Magistrates Court*. However, you have only recognised the correct answer from the alternatives.

By contrast, if I was to ask you to list the courts in the QLD court hierarchy from the lowest to the highest, and you answer (from memory) 'Magistrates Court, District Court, Supreme Court and High Court', you have retrieved the information from your memory and used it to answer the question.

The habit of answering questions using your memory is an outstanding way to test what you know and consolidate your learning.

Later in this chapter we will look at evidence suggesting that it is among the most powerful study approaches.

Beyond the Basics – Practice Questions and High Performance

Toward the end of 2022 I was fortunate enough to be part of an online seminar with Professor Mark McDaniel, one of the authors of a book about the science of learning called *Make it Stick*. He talked about the challenge of getting students to engage with the idea of using practice questions as part of their study routine. He said students found using practice questions more difficult than the more common but less effective study techniques such as re-reading notes or highlighting important work.

To my way of thinking, this poses a tremendous opportunity for motivated learners. The research we look at later in the chapter highlights using practice tests or questions as one of the top 2 study techniques. The other technique is spaced practice, which refers to looking back on work a number of times between first learning it and being tested on it – something we will explore as superhabit 6.

The opportunity for motivated learners is this: if most learners are going to settle for less-effective revision techniques like re-reading notes and creating summaries (both strategies that are considered low utility), then engaging with practice questions or tests that see you retrieving information is a unique opportunity to get ahead.

Practice questions and tests are generally not hard to find. Questions might be in textbooks and in the revision sheets handed out by teachers or, even better, you can write your own. We look at this concept later in the book around flashcards. We also look at the way mind maps can be used as a way of testing knowledge, another style of practice question.

Where Do We See this Habit in Other Environments?

In my time as a basketball coach, I have often heard the phrase 'You play how you practice'.

When I go down to watch my local professional basketball team, the Brisbane Bullets, train, they do so with tremendous intensity – often rehearsing specific sections of a game. For example, the training team might have 60 seconds on the clock, and be leading by 1 point, and have to finish the game from there.

They might then do the same drill, but this time starting with a 1-point deficit.

The point is that these drills are like practice questions – rehearsing exactly what the team has to do in a game situation, just like a student completing practice questions is rehearsing exactly what they have to do in an exam situation.

Any Boring Research to Support This?

One of the most commonly cited studies on study skills was put together by Dunlosky, Rawson, Marsh, Nathan and Willingham (2013), a group of educational researchers and practitioners. They considered 10 learning/study techniques that they saw as being relatively easy to use, and then sorted the techniques into the most effective (which they referred to as being high utility), moderately effective and those with low effectiveness (the low-utility learning/study techniques). The following diagram sets out their findings, with practice testing/practice questions among the 2 most effective study techniques. The other technique, distributed or spaced practice, refers to the benefits of coming back to revise work on multiple occasions between first learning the content and being tested on it. We will explore this idea further with superhabit 6.

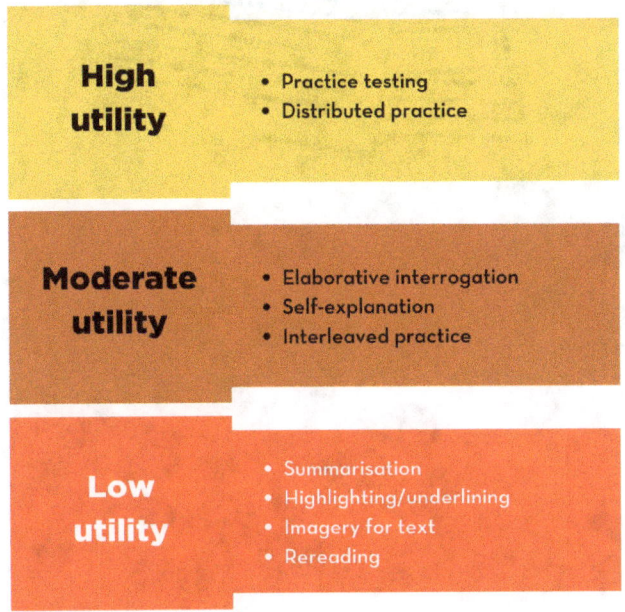

What is fascinating in this study are not just the more-effective strategies, but also the less-effective ones like re-reading, highlighting and making summaries. These strategies were included in the study because they are common strategies that students report using; however, they are not particularly effective.

If you are a student who relies on re-reading or highlighting for a significant amount of your study preparation, substituting the more effective strategy of doing practice questions or tests is worth considering.

A Final Word

Answering practice questions or practice tests that require you to retrieve information from your memory is an outstanding study habit. Answering questions from memory consolidates learning. Being able to identify questions you cannot yet answer gives you a focus for your future study. And, as a study technique that many students stop short of adopting, it can give you an advantage as an effective learner.

Superhabit 5

The High-Performance Habit of Sleep

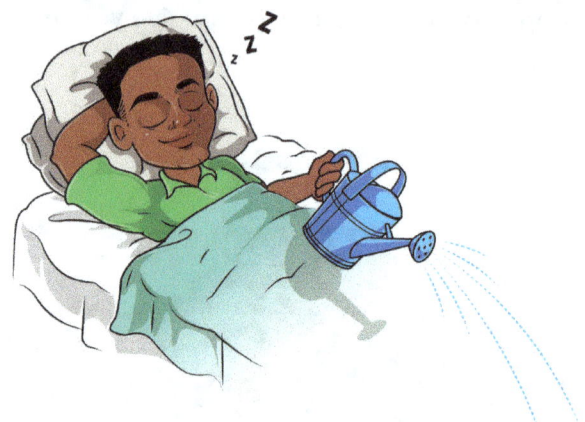

"Sleep is the most important 'repair' mechanism our body has, and getting enough of it will ensure you're feeling fit and energized the next day."

– Jason Smith

The Basics

The basics are simple:

1. You are going to be a more effective student with 8 to 10 hours of quality sleep on a regular basis.
2. Two key challenges to sleep are screens (phones, tablets and laptops) and caffeine (coffee, cola drinks and energy drinks). If you can turn off screens 30 to 60 minutes before bed and not drink caffeine in the late afternoon or evening, you are likely to improve your sleep quality.

VicHealth (2017) suggested that while teenagers need 8 to 10 hours of sleep per night, they were getting only 6.5 to 7.5 hours of sleep on average. How big a problem is this in terms of learning? Harvard University (2007) reminds us that adequate sleep each day is very important for learning and memory and that being sleep deprived reduces our ability to learn.

While considering the basics of sleep, Professor Michael Nagel (Francis and Nagel, 2020) from the University of the Sunshine Coast sets out a number of steps people can take to help with sleep, including:

1. Keep technology out of the bedroom (I remember hearing about a principal on the Gold Coast who felt so strongly about this that she bought all Year 12 students an old-fashioned alarm clock so they could use that to wake up and keep their mobile phone in another room).
2. Stop using devices/laptops in the evening, maybe around 9 pm, as they emit light that delays the onset of sleep.
3. Eat well and exercise.
4. Consider reading a book, meditating or doing a guided meditation or deep breathing if falling asleep is hard.

If you struggle to get enough sleep, this might be an issue worth discussing with an adult who might be able to help.

Beyond the Basics – Thinking Sleep and High-Performance

I want to propose a challenge to you, a challenge around high-performance study and sleep.

The challenge is this: just at the point of time when you need to be performing at your best with your academic study, completing assignments or preparing for exams, it is often more difficult to be getting enough sleep.

The pressure to study for exams and finish assignments means that we are often getting less sleep just as we need it most.

A paradox is a contradictory statement or position that is logically unacceptable, and I want to use the idea of the challenge of getting enough sleep during busy study times as a paradox, The Sleep-Study Paradox.

The Sleep-Study Paradox is that often we get the least sleep when we are engaged in our most important learning moments (around exams and assignments)

The paradox is that we are seeking our best academic performance while being sleep deprived, and later in this chapter we will look at research from university students that shows the more sleep they have the night before an exam, the better their results.

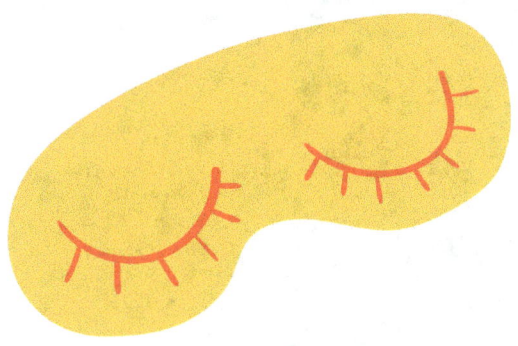

Where Do We See this Habit in Other Environments?

I often talk about one of the all-time great basketballers, LeBron James, as an example of another high-performance environment where sleep is crucial. LeBron James often discusses the importance of sleep to support his high-performance objectives. He describes the times you get those 8 or 9 hours of sleep as being 'amazing'.

For this chapter, I was interested to see if I could find a cultural example. Casey van Wensem (2016) is a composer and musician. He wrote an article listing the positive impacts of sleep on musicians and started by listing what good sleep protects against, including 'cognitive decline, altered mood, poorer motor skills, decreased motivation, and lack of initiative'.

He also mentioned that when we do not get enough sleep, we often don't recognise that we are being affected by a lack of sleep – others might notice, but we don't have insight into the problem.

The benefits of sleep for your brain that van Wensem (2016) lists include:

- consolidating memories
- supporting creating thinking
- making connections.

Both the problems that come from lack of sleep and the benefits of sleep listed in the context of a musician are just as relevant for students.

Any Boring Research to Support This?

Estevan, Sardi, Tejera, Silva and Tassino (2021) looked at the question of the impact of sleep on exam results in a paper titled 'Should I Study or Should I Go (to Sleep)?'

Their study of 349 students found that getting enough sleep the night before a test led to more correct answers on the exam.

It is a simple, but powerful, demonstration that adequate sleep helps academic performance in a real-life learning context (doing an exam).

A Final Word

Eight to 10 hours of sleep a night is going to make you feel better and perform better. If you make a habit of getting those 8 to 10 hours as often as you can, you give yourself the best chance of effective learning in class and as you study.

Superhabit 6
The High-Performance Habit of Spaced Practice

"Practice every time you get a chance."

— Bill Monroe, singer-songwriter (1911–96)

The Basics

Spaced practice is another study concept where an unfamiliar phrase has been used to explain a simple concept. Spaced practice, in the context of talking about study skills, refers to doing revision work between when you are taught something and when you are tested on it.

Another way of describing spaced practice is repeated exposure to content.

For example, most students learn a concept in class and perhaps do some homework on it that night. They then largely forget about the concept until the night before the exam, when they do some re-reading related to the topic, and the exam itself.

Spaced practice would include some revision of the material between the learning and cramming for the exam. This might involve creating a summary of the topic a week after seeing it in class and then coming back to the topic 4 weeks before the exam to create some flashcards, which are used for revision between then and the test.

Beyond the Basics – Thinking Spaced Practice and High-Performance

Spaced practice is one of the study habits that will set high-performing students apart from others, simply on the basis that most students will not get past the 'learn in class and cram before an exam' pattern of learning.

For an ambitious student, there are many opportunities to engage with content not just during the common teaching/pre-exam cramming times of learning. Opportunities you might consider to build some spaced practice into your routines include:

- pre-reading before a topic (this might just be a quick flick through the textbook to become familiar with key headings and terminology)
- going over content in class – being deliberate with notetaking and engaged with the work
- completing any homework questions
- about a week after the topic is covered, spend 10 minutes adding it to your mind map summary
- about 3 weeks after the topic, spend 10 minutes preparing some flashcard questions and answers, and use those for quick revision until the exam

- the week before the exam, quickly complete any revision activities the teacher gives you, so you can get feedback from them
- the night before the exam, re-read your mind map summary and work through your flashcards for the subject
- on the day of the exam, set aside 15 minutes to test your ability to recall knowledge by creating a mind map from memory and see if you need to brush up on any content you are uncertain about
- at any stage through the semester, a 'moment of gold' in terms of revision of material is if you find something in the media, such as a news article, or in your broader reading that links to your content. This provides both a point of revision and an opportunity to see the content you have learnt in another context.

Where Do We See this Habit in Other Environments?

If we look at other high-performance environments, whether sporting or musical, the idea of spaced practice becomes intuitively obvious.

Musicians don't build their ability by having an intense week of practice early in the year and another week before they perform – regular practice is what leads to high-performance outcomes.

Similarly, sporting teams don't do an intense week of training at the start of the pre-season and then again the week before their first game – regular practice is what leads to high-performance outcomes.

Any Boring Research to Support This?

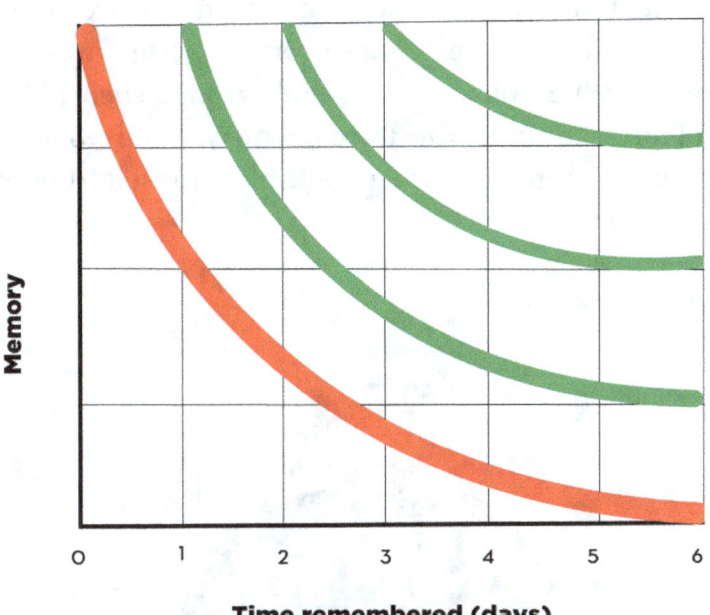

The core research behind spaced practice comes from more than 100 years ago, from a researcher named Hermann Ebbinghaus. The concept behind the forgetting curve is simple: every time you are actively exposed to content, you tend to forget it more slowly.

As simple and intuitive as this idea is, it is also the most basic idea behind success in study – the more times you engage with material, the better you will remember it.

Even if you are capable of getting good results through cramming the night before an exam, you will lose access to that material more quickly, meaning it will not form as effective a foundation for future challenges as it would for someone who made the effort to revise the content over time.

Carpenter, Cepeda, Rohrer, Kang and Pashler (2012) looked at the research behind spaced practice and found a number of studies that showed students who spaced their revision over time had better results. An example of these sorts of results was a study of students recalling history facts. Both groups spent the same amount of total time preparing the content, with the group using a spaced practice approach getting a 50% higher result – impressive given it took no extra time.

A Final Word

I suspect for most of us the notion that regular practice leads to high-performance outcomes makes sense. Focusing on what that means for our study, and the price we are prepared to pay to do some revision and preparation earlier than usual, will be useful in the quest for strong learning outcomes.

Superhabit 7
The High-Performance Habit of Weekly Planning and To-Do Lists

"An hour of planning can save you 10 hours of doing."
— Dale Carnegie,
American writer and lecturer (1888–1955)

The Basics

For this topic, the basics are indeed very basic.

Two planning tools – a weekly planner and to-do lists – can become allies in the busy world of learning.

The weekly planner is as it sounds, a plan of your time over the week, with time for study, time for hobbies, time for work and time for family and social commitments.

Douglas Barton, a researcher into the habits of successful students, gave a popular TED talk titled 'What Do Top Students Do Differently?'. In his talk he encouraged people to put the fun elements of life (like hobbies and social time) into their weekly planner, warning that people who filled their planner with only study commitments gave up on following them more quickly. Adding some fun activities made the planner more realistic, and easier to follow.

A to-do list is a place where you keep a record of the tasks you are working on. Some of the tasks – for example, an upcoming assignment – might be broken down into key steps, such as:

- understanding the task sheet, choosing a topic and planning the structure
- reading and research
- writing the draft
- using the feedback to write the final copy.

Beyond the Basics – a Weekly Planner, To-Do Lists and High Performance

As much as weekly planners and to-do lists are basic ideas, they can provide you with a significant advantage. They effectively provide you with a plan before you even have a challenge.

Let's illustrate that idea with an example. Let say as a student you are happily going about your week 4 of semester. During your accounting class, you are handed an assignment that you need to complete. Because you already have a weekly planner, you know that over the next 4 weeks you have time set aside to work on accounting. Perhaps you are given a little time in class to look at the assignment and break it down into several sections relevant to the task:

- research
- calculations
- writing a draft
- completing the final copy.

Very quickly you have two things that less-organised students will not have: a list of steps you need to work on to complete the task and a plan for when you have time set aside to do it.

One last comment here – just because you have the time set aside on the weekly planner does not mean you have to use it every week. Adapting your planner week by week, including weeks where events change your week dramatically, will help it be a realistic planning tool that works over time.

At a practical level a Word document with a table, or an Excel document, will allow you to set up a weekly planner (and there are plenty of online templates). To-do lists can be as simple as a list in a Word or Excel document, an exercise book or specially designed stationery. If you use an online tool, I suggest you highlight rather than delete completed tasks so you have a tangible reminder of progress.

Where Do We See this Habit in Other Environments?

Most of the examples linking study ideas to other high-performance environments have been related to music or sport. In this chapter we are going to look at a high-performance world of business, and what Richard Branson has to say about his use of lists as a planning tool.

In 2017 Richard Branson wrote a blog on his habit of using to-do lists, and his words are probably best in explaining how useful the habit is to him:

> *To say life as an entrepreneur and business leader is busy is an understatement. So, in order to make sure I achieve everything that not only needs to be done but also everything I want to get done, I make lists – lots of them.*
>
> *I have always lived my life by making lists.*
>
> *Every day I work through these lists. By ticking off each task, my ideas take shape and plans move forward.*

When Richard Branson talks about lists being a habit to cope with being busy, it is worth remembering that lives for students are often busy too – family, socialising, sports, music, work and hobbies are all competing for time. Setting up lists, ticking off tasks and seeing ambitions and plans take shape and move forward are as relevant for a student as they are for an entrepreneur.

Any Boring Research to Support This?

The core benefit I see form the use of a weekly planner and to-do list is that they easily combine to provide a plan when work needs to be done. However, research suggest that the benefits might be more profound than this, even helping with peace of mind.

Masicampo and Baumeister (2011) looked at the impact that having a plan toward a goal made to the thinking/worrying of people. They found that people who had set up a plan toward a goal did not spend as much time worrying about how they would achieve the goal; they tended to focus on the goal as they were directly working toward it.

The benefit of this is important. Students live busy lives, and to reduce the amount of worry about tasks we are not directly working on is a significant positive.

An article titled 'The Psychology of the To-Do List – Why Your Brain Loves Ordered Tasks' by Louise Chunn (2017) sets out three reasons why a to-do list might help us become more effective. They are:

1. A to-do list dampens anxiety about chaos (similar to the findings by Masicampo and Baumeister).
2. To-do lists give us structure to work through.
3. To-do lists give us proof that we are making progress and completing tasks as we tick them off our list or highlight them in a different colour.

In an article titled 'The Secret Psychology on Why We Love Completing To-Do Lists' Sara Davis set out another potential benefit of using to-do lists: the release of a feel-good chemical in the brain, dopamine. In Sara's words, 'When we complete individual tasks, our brains release dopamine which causes positive feelings such as happiness, pleasure, and motivation'.

A Final Word

The promise of using a weekly planner and a to-do list is simple. Rather than worrying about upcoming tasks, you immediately have a system to record what needs to be done and time set aside to do it. The alternative is distraction and stress about upcoming challenges being bigger than they need to be, and no hardworking student needs that.

Superhabit 8
The High-Performance Habit of a Deliberate Mindset

"The greatest discovery of my generation is that a human being can alter their life by altering the attitudes of mind."

– William James,
American philosopher (1842–1910)

The Basics

A mindset can be defined as the set of attitudes held by someone.

As learners, we have choices about our attitude toward learning. For learners interested in the high-performance aspects of effective learning, I want to propose three different models of deliberate attitudes (mindsets) that might influence your mindset on your study journey.

The basics of these three models are as follows:

- **Growth mindset:** A growth mindset encourages us to lean into challenging work and reminds us that persisting with challenging work is what grows our capacity.
- **Grit:** Grit is the perseverance towards long term goals.
- **Hard choices:** This is a framework for deciding 'who I want to be' in moments of deciding between two options that both have benefits (for example, the hard choice between a fun afternoon at the movies or a productive afternoon of study).

Beyond the Basics – Thinking Mindset and High Performance

Even before we start further exploring these three mindset ideas, it is worth acknowledging that we are only going to touch briefly on each idea. However, each of the three mindset ideas I am presenting to you here are from researchers and authors who happen to have brilliant TED talks. My suggestion is to use this chapter for some background and then watch the following TED talks to build your interest and understanding.

- **Growth mindset** – Carol Dweck, 'The Power of Believing You Can Improve'
- **Grit** – Angela Duckworth, 'Grit: The Power of Passion and Perseverance'
- **Hard choices** – Ruth Chang, 'How to Make Hard Choices'

Let's start by looking at the research from Carol Dweck, Professor of Psychology at Stanford University. Her interest is around the idea of a growth mindset – that is, that there is a specific set of ideas that people who learn more hold. The idea stems from observations that people who say 'I love a challenge' when confronted with difficult work, rather than giving up or finding reasons why they cannot do it, do better as learners.

According to Dweck (2006), the reason people succeed is not because they are more talented, but because they believe in their ability to improve, they persist, they try different strategies and, following effort, they do improve.

As a student, when you make mistake, get a poor result or feel like giving up it is a key 'moment of truth'. If you can find the mindset to try another approach to solve the problem, persist, and recognise that being at the point of making mistakes and frustration (feeling like giving up) is the point at which you can build your capacity if you persist, then your mindset will become more robust for learning.

In a similar research mode, Angela Duckworth, a former high school maths teacher and Professor of Psychology at University of Pennsylvania found that it was not IQ or family background that was behind success, it was something she described as grit, which was the passion and perseverance to work toward long-term goals, sticking with your future day in and day out while working hard (Duckworth, 2013).

It is interesting to link this research and the idea of grit (working over time toward long-term goals) with some of the research of John Hattie, an education researcher who in 2017 ranked the impact of 252 different influences on learning. Prior ability/prior learning had the 9th biggest effect on learning, suggesting that if we can set a high standard with our study and learning over time, that will build a stronger foundation for future learning and positively impact future results. However, it is only though sticking with long-term goals, or grit, that we will see the most significant impacts.

The third and final mindset idea that I want to introduce is around hard choices – making a choice between two alternatives that are both better in some ways.

For example, consider the choice on a Saturday afternoon between going to watch a movie with a friend or staying home to do some study. Both have benefits, a social, fun afternoon versus getting some study done. So how can you make a choice?

Ruth Chang (2016) suggests that these hard choices are interesting because they give us an opportunity to decide 'Here is who I am' with the choice.

Early in a term, you might decide that the 'who I am' choice is to be a friend and enjoy a social outing. At another time in the term, the 'who I am' choice might favour being a student with academic goals, and you might stay home and get some study done.

These three ideas – growth mindset, grit and hard choices – start to provide some ideas as to how we can be deliberate about our mindset.

Where Do We See this Habit in Other Environments?

Most years my wife, Sam, and I travel to New York for the Christmas holidays, swapping the heat of Queensland for the occasional snow of a northern hemisphere winter. Each visit we walk over the Brooklyn Bridge and enjoy the views of Manhattan.

Washington Roebling was a civil engineer who supervised the construction of the bridge as chief engineer from 1869. In 1970 a fire broke out on the bridge and, in the process of fighting the fire, Roebling ended up with decompression sickness. However, he did not give up on the project and, with the help of his wife, Emily, remotely managed the project to see the bridge built.

Rather than give up when his health was poor, Roebling's mindset of perseverance, coupled with his wife's work, saw the bridge opened in 1883.

Any Boring Research to Support This?

Carol Dweck, Ruth Chang and Angela Duckworth are all researchers who have studied their particular area of interest in growth mindset, hard choices and grit.

Each of these ideas provides a specific approach to a deliberate mindset, whether it be around the value of choosing to persevere where mistakes are made or hard work is encountered (growth mindset), the importance of working toward long-term goals over time (grit), or the importance of being deliberate around decisions where two options both have benefits (hard choices).

A Final Word

There is a quote on this topic that I particularly like by William James (1842–1910):

> *The greatest discovery of my generation is that a human being can alter their life by altering the attitudes of mind.*

For a student ambitious about being as effective as they can be as a learner, thinking about the idea of mindset and how it might support their efforts has value.

Habits in Practice
A Deliberate Technique for Exams and Assignments

"An amazing performance is always a reflection of awesome amounts of practice."

– Robin Sharma,
Canadian author

What Does the Study Habit of a Deliberate Technique for Exams and Assignments Look Like?

One of my indulgences in life is to buy front-row tickets to watch my local professional basketball team, the Brisbane Bullets. Before the game there is a function, and we often arrive a bit more than an hour before the game. It is interesting to watch the players from both teams as they go through their pre-game routines – some shooting, some dribbling the basketball, some doing visualisation routines, some sitting quietly, some talking to coaches, some stretching. The 12 players in each team all have their own deliberate approach to being ready to perform at their best come game time.

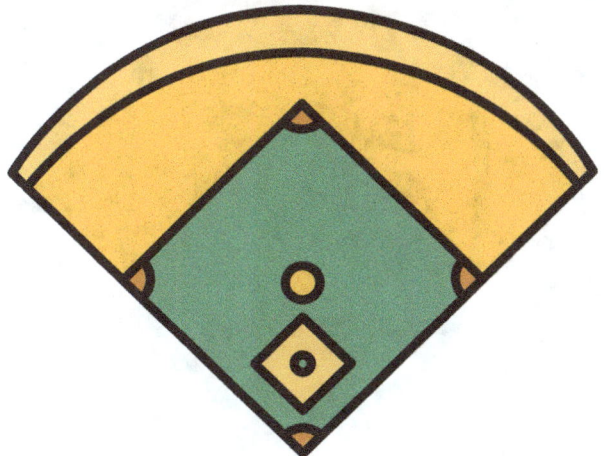

That is what this chapter is about – building routines that will support us to perform at our best when it comes to the study 'game time' of completing exams or assignments. If we want to be high-performing students, it stands to reason that we should think about building routines that might support us in getting there.

Let's consider the high-performance challenge of an exam. The challenge here is in the one, two or three hours of an exam where we want to be doing quality work – recalling as much as we can, answering questions without too much stress and progressing through the challenge of the exam successfully. We can probably recognise that there are multiple steps we can take to help with this, from being well rested to having resources organised and calmly revising material prior to the exam.

The high-performance challenge of an assignment is different. The challenge here might be around starting early enough to become a subject expert, using this subject knowledge to build on great ideas, seeking and incorporating feedback and having enough time to format and proofread the final copy.

How Might a Deliberate Technique for Exams and Assignments Support My Study?

This is a topic that, as an ambitious student, you are going to have to build into a plan that best suits you. Let's start by looking at some elements you might put into an exam routine, which I have set out as several possible steps for consideration:

Step 1 – A good night's sleep: Set yourself the challenge of getting to bed at a reasonable hour so you are rested and ready to perform on the day.

Step 2 – One last revision of the content: In the hour before the exam, sit down and jot down, from memory, a mind map of the content for the exam. This is a great way to remind yourself of what you have covered and check if there are any last-minute knowledge gaps you need to work on.

Step 3 – Move a little: A 10- to 20-minute walk before an exam is a great way to have your brain ready for the challenge. The short-term benefits of exercise include improved mood and focus, and that makes it a great pre-exam activity (Francis and Nagel, 2000).

Step 4 – Do some warm-up questions: Keep a few flashcards of important questions with you, and do these questions before the exam. Just like an athlete or musician does a warm-up by practising part of their performance, this is a great way to get ready to perform in the exam.

Step 5 – Use a little superstition: Lucky socks or a lucky pen might be a fun way to engage with performance – and if you ever end up having a poor exam, you can substitute in some new lucky pens or socks as a way of getting ready for the next challenge.

Step 6 – Set a clear goal for the exam: About 15 minutes before an exam, you might choose to sit down and write a process goal.

In this book we have already looked at SMART and open goals; a process goal is another sort of goal that focuses on what you can control over the period of the exam. I think it is a great way to not get too concerned about how much you do or don't know during the exam, instead moving your focus to how well you will work during the period of the exam.

Process goals might relate to:

- carefully managing time
- reading questions carefully
- planning answers
- working with intensity for the full time of the exam.

Professor Michael Nagel, when writing about the idea of an exam routine, says that routine is something that the human brain thrives on. Taking the time to develop an exam routine that works well for us is a step to consider as you look to get the most out of yourself as a learner (Francis and Nagel, 2020).

Having looked at an exam routine, we move to building an approach for tackling assignments.

I don't think anyone will be shocked when I say the key concept here is managing procrastination – or, perhaps with an appropriately passive-aggressive tone, getting ahead of procrastination.

I suspect that almost all students are familiar with the feeling of putting assignment work off until it becomes a last minute 'sprint' to upload something that is less than what it could be, just before the assignment's due time.

This leads to the three core problems, as I see them, with leaving assignments until the last minute:

1. We do not get the chance to become a subject expert through reading widely.
2. We do not get the chance to incorporate feedback and revision into our work (this includes if there is a formal drafting process and we hand in a poor-quality draft that only allows for feedback on our poor-quality work).
3. Working at the last minute is often stressful and does not allow us to be as creative as we otherwise might be.

As you think about the elements in your assignment routine, here are some ideas worth considering:

Step 1 – Start early and understand the assignment topic: This could be a challenge to complete on the day the task sheet is released.

Step 2 – Become confident with the subject: Use that understanding of the assignment topic to find a few great articles/readings, and become confident with the topic – a subject/topic expert.

Step 3 – Set aside some quality time: Find some time to work when you are rested and comfortable enough to be able to give the assignment the focus it deserves. For school students, weekends are often a great time for this.

Step 4 – Set an anti-procrastination goal: Challenge yourself with the halfway point of the timeline. Can you make useful progress before you get to this halfway point? (That is, if you have 4 weeks for an assignment, stop at the 2-week mark to consider how much progress you have made).

Step 5 – Prepare to finish strongly: Break the assignment into steps, with deliberate time set aside for revising and improving the draft to ensure you finish well.

Step 6 – Learn from the assignment feedback: The best approach to feedback that I have seen was a student who carried an exercise book with her and jotted down any draft or assignment feedback that she received in the book. This gave her some great data to work toward improving her approach to assignments.

Which Superhabits Does Having a Deliberate Plan for Exams and Assignments Support?

Building an effective exam routine might incorporate the habit of **setting goals**, especially a process goal to guide your efforts during the exam. It might also include the habit of **practice questions** as part of a 'warm-up', harness the habit of **sleep** to prepare for the exam and use the habit of **mindset** as you create a deliberate approach to your exam routine.

Building an effective assignment routine might include the habit of **spaced practice** (especially starting early), the habit of **sleep** in finding some time to work on the assignment when you are well rested and the habits of both **setting goals** and **using to-do lists** to break the assignment into smaller pieces and enjoy your progress through them.

A Final Word

Building routines that you can trust around exams and assignments will support high-performance academic outcomes. In the same way performers and athletes have routines that see them perform at their best, you can build these habits to support your ambitions and performance as a student.

Habits in Practice
From the Pomodoro Technique to 'Flow'

"Flow is being completely involved in an activity for its own sake. The ego falls away. Time flies. Every action, movement, and thought follows inevitably from the previous one, like playing jazz."
– Mihaly Csikszentmihalyi, Hungarian-American psychologist (1934–2021)

What Do the Study Habits of the Pomodoro Technique and Flow Look Like in Practice?

This chapter looks at two somewhat contrasting states of study.

The first is the pomodoro technique. This involves relatively short bursts of focused study of around 15 to 25 minutes, flowed by a short 5-minute break. I think this is a great approach to study when you are tired or lacking a little motivation to get started. For each 15- to 25-minute study block you have a key objective or goal in mind (for example, *I am going to complete the maths questions in chapter 3*), and you find an area where there will be no distractions for that period of time (ideally with your email shut down, social media off and phone in the next room).

'Flow' is the state of being completely engaged in an activity, when the work is enjoyable and when the focus is on achieving something difficult and worthwhile. A key researcher into the concept of flow is Mihaly Csikszentmihalyi, whose quote starts this chapter.

Many people are familiar with the idea of flow from hearing athletes talk about their performance when they were 'in the zone' – when a level of focus and engagement made high-quality performance come easily. This brings us back to the idea of flow and study. Wouldn't it be great if study could come easily and in a highly focused way?

Ransom Patterson (2018), in an article titled 'The Flow State: How to Enter Your Brain's Most Productive State', wrote about the idea of flow and study, referencing Csikszentmihalyi's work.

He suggested that as well as engagement in our work, which is not always easy when we are studying topics we may not have control over, elements that help move us toward a state of flow include:

- not being hungry
- cutting out distractions
- using the pomodoro technique
- single-tasking
- getting enough sleep
- being comfortable.

This list, linked to the concept of flow, is a great checklist of your readiness for study.

How Might the Pomodoro Technique and Flow Support My Study?

There is a very simple quote that I like: 'Fake it until you make it'.

I see the pomodoro technique as being the 'fake it until you make it' study approach. Often on weekdays people do their study in the evenings, after a day of classes, perhaps some sport, musical activities or a job. When you come to get some study done your brain has worked hard for the day, you are feeling a little tired and the motivation is not what it could be.

The pomodoro technique allows you to make a little deal with yourself: *I am going to set a timer for 20 minutes of work, leave my phone in the next room and set an academic task – for example, finding 3 relevant sources for an upcoming assignment.* Twenty minutes of work is not a huge ask, and then you can have a break and a quick snack and catch up with friends, and onto your next 20 minutes, having already ticked off some progress. Fifteen to 25 minutes is about the length of our attention span, and breaking work into 'chunks' of this size allows us to work within this span.

Working toward achieving a flow state with study is something I see more aligned with weekend work, where you have little else on during a day, or perhaps during an exam block when there are no classes and your only focus is to get some study done. You can start your work well rested and comfortable, minimise distractions and look to engage with your work and be creative. This is part of the reason I think weekends are a great time to consider working on assignments, allowing you a higher level of focus and creativity supporting these tasks.

The concept of a flow state is another reason that starting assignment work early has value. Being ahead on a task is more likely to see you enjoying working on it, being creative and seeing easy progress compared to being behind and feeling the pressure to finish.

Which Superhabits Do the Pomodoro Technique and Flow Support?

The habit of **single-tasking** is explicitly part of both the pomodoro technique and the concept of flow, reminding us of its importance as a study habit. The habit of **sleep** is an important element in finding a state of flow with work, just as the habit of starting with a **goal** in mind is an important part of each pomodoro session. To set up the environment that supports either the pomodoro technique or a state of flow, the habit of a **deliberate mindset** is needed to find the right environment, manage distractions and work out the intent of the study session. Finally, the habit of **spaced practice**, or starting early on work, allows work on an assignment without the stress of deadlines eating into the sense of flow.

A Final Word

This chapter provides you with two very specific ways of working. The pomodoro technique allows you to set an objective (a mini goal), manage distractions, work effectively for small amounts of time, have a break, and then do it again. This is a great recipe for getting work done when you are a little tired.

Looking to study in a flow state requires us to be deliberate in our approach to getting ready to study, be engaged with our work, manage distractions, start early on work and be well rested. It is a great concept which supports the idea of setting aside time on a day when not much else is on to become engaged in assignment work.

Habits in Practice
Learning from Feedback

"We all need people who give us feedback. That's how we improve."
– Bill Gates,
co-founder of Microsoft

What Does the Study Habit of Learning from Feedback Look Like in Practice?

I want to start with some research that we as teachers often come across and think about what it might mean from a student perspective. As teachers, we are often told that one of the most important things we can do to support learning is to give students quality feedback about their work.

One of the foremost education researchers, John Hattie (2009), found that giving students feedback had an effect size of 0.73. The 'effect size' is a measure of the value of a strategy, and feedback's effect size of 0.73 has almost double the impact of what Hattie considered an effective strategy of 0.4 – effectively showing that feedback is important to learning.

Let's turn this around.

If one of the most effective strategies for teachers is to provide feedback, then it stands to reason that one of the most effective strategies for students is to engage with and learn from feedback. Feedback can be accessed in many forms, including from peers, teachers and other people prepared to read and comment on an assignment. Many schools and some universities provide draft feedback, and starting early on an assignment to hand in a thorough draft and get feedback to improve it is a great strategy.

How Might a Deliberate Technique for Learning from Feedback Support My Study?

Feedback comes at different times across the year – feedback on drafts, feedback on assignments, practice exams, exams and report cards.

The first step in making learning from feedback part of what you do is to have a mindset that looks for and appreciates feedback. This can be particularly challenging when feedback comes as the same time as marks are released and the focus is on the marks (and the emotions that come with a good or bad results) rather than the feedback.

The best idea I have seen in practice around putting feedback together was a student who had an exercise book where she wrote down feedback from each assignment and exam. Not only did the exercise book help her put together her feedback, it also encouraged her to ask questions about what she did not understand. Recording feedback across subjects in the one book allowed her to see any patterns in her work where she could improve.

Which Superhabits Does Having a Deliberate Plan for Learning from Feedback Support

Learning from feedback is all about choosing a **deliberate mindset**, where you acknowledge the importance of feedback to learning. The first step is to acknowledge that feedback is important and to learn from feedback when you receive it (which can be difficult when a grade and feedback come at the same time). The next high-performance step might be to take the time to put the feedback you receive in the one place and learn from it over time.

A Final Word

If feedback is something that teachers are told is important in positively impacting student results, it stands to reason that it is important for students to make the most of feedback too, particularly those students focused on high-performance study results.

Habits in Practice
Mind Maps and Flashcards

"Don't practice until you get it right, practice until you never get it wrong."

— John Flanagan,
Australian author

What Does the Study Habit of Mind Maps and Flashcards Look Like in Practice?

In this chapter we are examining two very specific study approaches: using mind maps and flashcards as study aids.

Let's start with mind maps. I suspect as experienced students you will have seen and probably used mind maps. They are a way of organising information with the key topic in the middle of a page, then the key subheadings expanding out from there with information about each subheading.

Mind maps provide a way of organising information as a diagram rather than a block of text. They also allow levels of information to be emphasised, and connections between information can be noted. Put simply, they are an effective way of organising information graphically that seems to help with the recall of the information later.

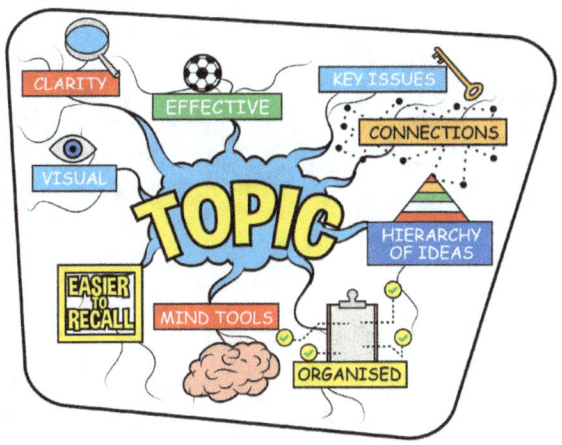

Flashcards well and truly sit in the 'oldie but a goodie' section of study ideas. The idea is simple. You use index cards or smaller pieces of paper and write a question on one side of the paper and the answer to the question on the other. You then have a surprisingly powerful learning aid, which you can use to test your knowledge of a topic over time.

How Do Mind Maps and Flashcards Support My Study?

There are two applications for mind maps that make them a valuable study aid. The first is as a method to summarise content. Going through a chapter of a textbook, for example, and summarising the information in a mind map is a great first step in gathering the information you need to learn for a topic.

A second application of mind maps is as a retrieval activity. Previously we talked about the value of retrieval practice for students – consolidating memories by effectively recalling information from your memory. Setting up a mind map for a topic and writing down everything you know on the topic in the form of a mind map is a great test of what you know. In the chapter on exam techniques, this is suggested as a possible strategy for one of the last steps before an exam – write down everything that you can recall on the topic, and check if you are missing any information.

Flashcards are a study technique that align with several key study ideas. You can write the questions and answers on your flashcards over the course of a term or semester, gradually building your stock of questions. Flashcards then allow you to give yourself a practice test, or what you now know as a spaced-practice revision activity.

One challenge with using flashcards is the 'illusion of knowledge'. Flashcards can be a passive study technique, where you read the question, then the answer, and assume you are on the right track because the answer seems familiar. Using flashcards in this way has not forced you to recall the information from your memory. Instead, taking the time to read the flashcard, jotting down an answer and then checking the answer on the back of the card is a more active way of assessing your memory.

The source of questions to make up flashcards can be broad – from textbooks to revision materials your teacher gives you, questions you cover in class and questions you make up yourself.

I want to add one further possible use of flashcards. One study technique that is shown to have benefits has the impressive name 'interleaved practice'. What the technique suggests is that if you move between different types of revision questions, you will get a better learning result than if you just focus on one type of question.

For example, let's say that in a semester of maths you have studied the topics of geography, percentages and probability. If you review by asking yourself a bunch of questions on geography, then a bunch of questions on percentages and then a bunch of questions on probability, that is reasonable. However, a better way is to mix the questions up, moving between the topics.

Having some flashcards and mixing them up is a simple way to create interleaved practice and can even be done by mixing flashcards across subjects.

Which Superhabits Does Using Mind Maps and Flashcards Support?

Both mind maps and flashcards give you a specific method of starting revision early, which is the core concept behind the habit of **spaced practice**. They are also sources of **practice tests and questions**, another key learning habit. Mind maps can be used as a practice question when you recall and create a mind map about the information from a topic. Both the use of mind maps and flashcards require a **deliberate mindset** to put them into practice as study ideas.

A Final Word

Mind maps and flashcards are two practical study ideas that, with effort, can support students with their high-performance ambitions.

Habits in Practice
Challenging Procrastination

"My advice is to never do tomorrow what you can do today. Procrastination is the thief of time."

– Charles Dickens,
English author (1812–70)

What Does the Study of Challenging Procrastination Look Like in Practice?

Amy Novotny (2010) identified that between 80% and 95% of university students procrastinate and, given that it is one of the most common challenges students talk about regarding study, this is not a surprising figure.

That makes it a study challenge worth engaging with in a thoughtful way.

There are already ideas that you have been introduced to in this book that might help you move past procrastination, including using the pomodoro technique to get started when study seems challenging.

How Might a Deliberate Technique of Challenging Procrastination Support My Study?

There are two elements that I want to look at in this section: an idea for challenging procrastination around assignments and then some thoughts from Randall Munroe on getting past procrastination.

Assignments are a classic breeding ground of procrastination – the last-minute flurry of activity to submit or upload an assignment moments before it is due is one of the cliches of student life.

As a postgraduate business student who had a tendency to procrastinate, I came across a business model that described the progress groups made toward an objective called the punctuated-equilibrium model. The model says that for the first half of the project time the group accomplishes very little (almost like they have procrastinated). In the second half of the time they become effective and make progress toward their goal, sometimes with a last-minute increase in productivity.

As a model of group performance it has little relevance to study – except in this one way. The idea of a group, or individual, making little to no progress in the first half of a task seems to me to be the ideal benchmark to use to build the habit of challenging procrastination.

Here is the anti-procrastination challenge I want to put to you: take an assignment that you want to focus on, and then calculate the halfway point between the date you received the assignment and the due date. For example, for a four-week assignment the halfway point will be at two weeks. Your challenge is to have made effective progress on the assignment by that halfway point. If you are successful, you will have struck a blow against the tendency to procrastinate, and my suspicion is that you will be ahead of many of your peers.

The second idea I want to share in this section is from Tim Urban (2016), who gave a TED talk titled 'Inside the Mind of a Master Procrastinator'. It is a brilliant talk and makes compelling and entertaining viewing.

Tim doesn't give a complete answer to procrastination, rather he introduces three characters in our brain who are part of the interplay of procrastination. He then provides a framework for understanding and challenging the characters involved in the process of procrastination.

The first character is the rational decision-maker, whose general encouragement is to make rational decisions to be productive.

The second character is the instant gratification monkey, whose advice is to live in the moment and do whatever seems to be fun at the time, from watching videos to getting a snack.

The third character is the one that gets things done for a procrastinator, the panic monster. Importantly, the instant gratification monkey is scared of the panic monster. The panic monster wakes up when an important deadline is getting close, and in a flurry of activity gets things done in the nick of time.

Procrastinator's Brain

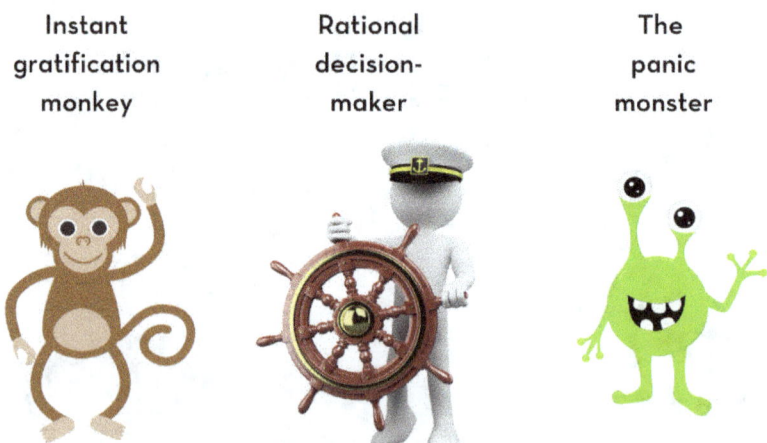

| Instant gratification monkey | Rational decision-maker | The panic monster |

Tim finishes his talk with a challenge that involves thinking about someone living for 90 years. To conceptualise the lifespan of 90 years, he uses a box to represent every week over those 90 years, commenting that those boxes make up a whole life and that, with some boxes already in the past, not a huge number of boxes/weeks remain. This leads to his challenge, in his words:

> *We need to think about what we're really procrastinating on, because everyone is procrastinating on something in life. We need to stay aware of the Instant Gratification Monkey. That's a job for all of us. And because there's not that many boxes on there, it's a job that should probably start today.*

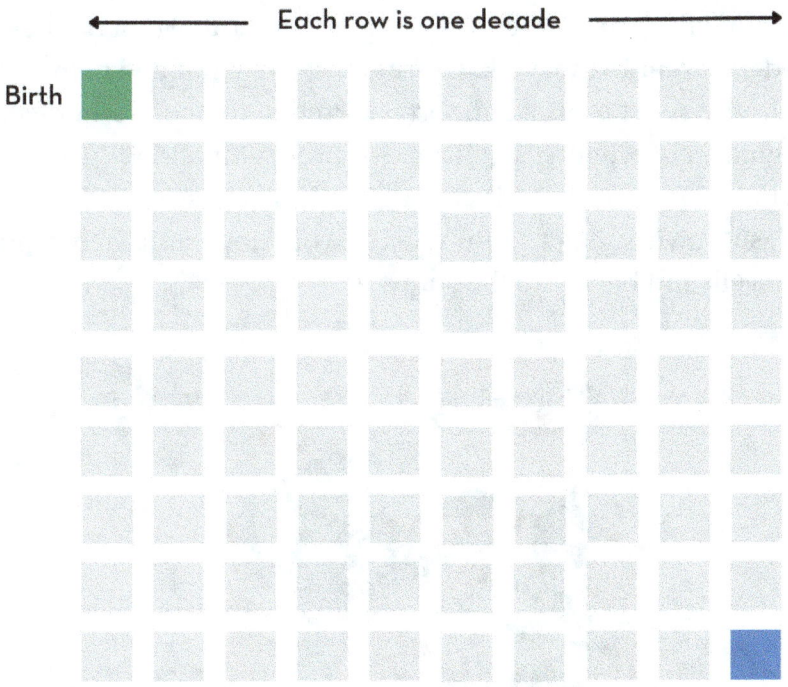

Which Superhabits Does Challenging Procrastination Support?

Challenging procrastination starts with a **deliberate mindset**, choosing to engage with work earlier than you otherwise would. It supports the habit of **spaced practice**, which focuses on starting tasks earlier than you otherwise would. It is supported by the habit of **single-tasking**, as it is the distractions that draw us away from the work. Finally, it encourages us to use active study techniques like **practice questions and tests** (for example, making and revising with flashcards) throughout a unit of work.

I want to sneak a semi-superhabit in here, something that has been referred to earlier in the book. **Exercise** is a great habit to help with study. In the short term it supports alertness, memory and focus. It is a great tool when struggling with procrastination – use it to have a break from study and refocus. Or, if you are struggling to get started, sit down and get 15 minutes of work done and then go for a quick walk and back into the study.

A Final Word

Procrastination is a challenge that the quote at the start of this chapter demonstrates goes back centuries.

If you are prepared to be conscious of the challenge of procrastination, try different approaches to get started earlier on your work and find a strategy that works for you. You will give yourself another advantage as you look to perform at a high level as a student.

References

Carpenter, S. K. (2012). 'Using Spacing to Enhance Diverse Forms of Learning'. *Educational Psychology Review*, 369–378.

Chang, R. (2016). 'How to Make Hard Choices'. (Video). Retrieved from TED website: https://www.ted.com/talks/ruth_chang_how_to_make_hard_choices?language=en

Chunn, L. (2017, May 10). 'The Psychology of the To-do List – Why your Brain Loves Ordered Tasks'. Retrieved from *The Guardian*: https://www.theguardian.com/lifeandstyle/2017/may/10/the-psychology-of-the-to-do-list-why-your-brain-loves-ordered-tasks

Davis, S. (2022, May 11). 'The Secret Psychology on Why We Love Completing To-Do Lists'. Retrieved from Workast website: https://www.workast.com/blog/the-secret-psychology-on-why-we-love-completing-to-do-lists/#

Duckworth, A. (2013, May). 'Grit: The Power of Passion and Perseverance'. (Video). Retrieved from TED Conferences website: https://www.ted.com/talks/angela_lee_duckworth_grit_the_power_of_passion_and_perseverance?language=en

Dunlosky J, et al. (2013). 'Improving Students' Learning With Effective Learning Techniques: Promising Directions From Cognitive and Educational Psychology'. *Psychological Scieince in the Public Interest*, 4–58.

Dweck, C. (2006). *Mindset: The New Psychology of Success*. New York: Ballentine Books.

Egay, F. (2022, October 31). 'The Most Important Story About Goal Setting'. Retrieved from Inspirationalife website: https://inspirationalife.com/story-about-goal-setting/

Estevan I, S. R. (2021). 'Should I Study or Should I Go (To Sleep)? The Influence of Test Schedule on the Sleep Behavior of Undergraduates and its Association with Performance'. *PLoS ONE*, 1–9.

Francis, S., & Nagel, M. (2020). *Your High-Performance Guide to Study and Learning*. Melbourne: Hawker Brownlow Education.

Harvard Medical School. (2007). 'Sleep, Learning and Memory'. Retrieved from Harvard Medical School website: https://healthysleep.med.harvard.edu/healthy/matters/benefits-of-sleep/learning-memory

Hattie, J. (2009). *Visible Learning*. London: Routledge.

Kassarnig V, et al (2017). 'Class Attendance, Peer Similarity, and Academic Performance in a Large Field Study'. *PLoS ONE*, 1–15.

Klickstein, G. (2009, December 19). 'Habits of Excellence'. Retrieved from *Musicians Way*: https://www.musiciansway.com/blog/2009/12/habits-of-excellence/

Locke, E. A. (2002). 'Building a Practically Useful Theory of Goal Setting and Task Motivation: A 35-Year Odyssey'. *American Psychologist*, 705–717.

Masicampo, E. J., & Baumeister, R. F. (2011). 'Consider It Done! Plan Making Can Eliminate the Cognitive Effects of Unfulfilled Goals'. *Journal of Personality and Social Psychology*, 667–683.

Miller, T. (2020, December 15). 'Harnessing Your Highest Potential in Performance'. Retrieved from *Better Humans*: https://betterhumans.pub/harnessing-your-highest-potential-in-performance-5763201eb600

Mueller, P. & Oppenheimer, D. M. (2014). 'The Pen Is Mightier Than the Keyboard: Advantages of Longhand Over Laptop Note Taking'. Retrieved from *Psychological Science*: https://journals.sagepub.com/doi/abs/10.1177/0956797614524581

Murphy, M. (2018, April 15). 'Neuroscience Explains Why You Need To Write Down Your Goals If You Actually Want To Achieve Them'. Retrieved from *Forbes*: https://www.forbes.com/sites/markmurphy/2018/04/15/neuroscience-explains-why-you-need-to-write-down-your-goals-if-you-actually-want-to-achieve-them/?sh=11429ee67905

Novotny, A. (2010, January). 'Procrastination or "Intentional Delay"?' Retrieved from *American Psychological Association*: https://www.apa.org/gradpsych/2010/01/procrastination

Patterson, R. (2018, April 17). 'The Flow State: How to Enter Your Brain's Most Productive State'. Retrieved from College Info Geek website: https://collegeinfogeek.com/flow/

Urban, T. (2016). 'Inside the Mind of a Master Procrastinator'. Retrieved from TED website: https://www.ted.com/talks/tim_urban_inside_the_mind_of_a_master_procrastinator/transcript?language=en

van Wensem, C. (2016, August 24). 'The Scientific Truth About How Sleep Affects Your Practice Sessions and Performances'. Retrieved from Sonicbids website: https://blog.sonicbids.com/why-a-good-nights-sleep-could-be-your-best-practice-and-performance-tool

VicHealth. (2017). *Sleep and Mental Wellbeing: Exploring the Links*. Retrieved from VicHealth website.

Ward, A., Duke, K., Gneezy, A., & Bos, M. (2017). 'Brain Drain: The Mere Presence of One's Own Smartphone Reduces Available Cognitive Capacity'. *The Consumer in a Connected World*, 140–154.

www.ingramcontent.com/pod-product-compliance
Lightning Source LLC
Chambersburg PA
CBHW050259120526
44590CB00016B/2415